IMAGES OF ENGLAND

# AROUND
# STAFFORD

The High House, decorated for George VI's Coronation, 1937. Like other shopkeepers in the main street, William Marson of the High House decorated his shop front with flags and garlands for the Coronation. Tall blue poles were erected in red and white tubs at twenty-five yard intervals from Gaol Square to The Grapes public house corner. Red, white and blue garlands and pennants were suspended from these.

IMAGES OF ENGLAND

# AROUND STAFFORD

ROY LEWIS

The
History
Press

First published in 1999 by Tempus Publishing
Reprinted 2004

Reprinted in 2008 by
The History Press
The Mill, Brimscombe Port,
Stroud, Gloucestershire, GL5 2QG
www.thehistorypress.co.uk

Reprinted 2012

ISBN 978 0 7524 1811 7

Typesetting and origination by
Tempus Publishing Limited
Printed and bound in England

*For Gareth and Louise.*

*Front cover:* Siemens Bros' factory, Stafford, 1907. Pre-formed coils are
being wound into stators of low voltage electric motors.

Police lorries, 1926. These Albion lorries belonging to the Staffordshire County Police were photographed while their drivers were on stand-by at Stafford to deal with any disturbances arising from the General Strike. In Stafford itself they were only called upon to arrest Councillor Tom Roberts when he was leading a picket to stop lorries on the A34 north of the town.

# Contents

# Acknowledgements

To all who have written about Stafford and district in the past, to librarians, archivists, museum curators, local historians and all who have shared their knowledge with me, I acknowledge my debt and my gratitude. They have made writing this book a journey of discovery and pleasure. I hope readers will share this with me.

Acknowledgement is also made to all those who have allowed their photographs and postcards to be reproduced. Some photographs have always existed in several prints and some are modern copies of older photographs. Although every effort has been made to trace the holder of the original photograph, these efforts are not always successful and I apologise to anyone omitted from the list below.

The following hold the photographs and postcards included in this book and have allowed them to be copied. Numbers refer to pages and A and B to upper and lower illustrations respectively.

Staffordshire Arts and Museum Service: 4, 10B, 16A, 23A, 26, 28B, 51A, 52, 54A, 64A, 64B, 65A, 65B, 66, 67A, 67B, 68B, 69A, 69B, 70A, 82A, 86B, 87A, 88B, 91B, 92B, 94, 95A, 95B, 96, 100B, 101, 102A, 102B, 103A, 103B, 104B, 105A, 105B, 106A, 106B, 107A, 107B, 108A, 109A, 109B, 116, 117B. Staffordshire County Record Office: 70B, 71A, 71B, 72A. Staffordshire County Education Department Quality Learning Services Support Unit: 2, 4, 10A, 12A, 27A, 30B, 33B, 39B, 43A, 45A, 55B, 73, 80B, 99A, 99B, 108B, 114A, 115, 118B. Staffordshire County Library: 9, 41B. Stafford Historical and Civic Society: 12A, 20, 30B, 33B, 45A, 55B. Englesea Brook Museum of Primitive Methodism: 92A. Staffordshire Newsletter: 21A, 43B. John Wheeldon Primary School: 99B. C. Ecclestone: 33A, 36A, 49A. Mrs G. El Balbisi: 38, 39A, 58B, 86A. Mr A. Clarke: 41A. Evode Ltd: 114A. Revd M. Fisher: 87B. Mrs N. Gilden: 32B. R. Horsley: 62A. E. Loveys: 45B, 98B. Mrs D. Machin: 35A. Mrs A. Middleton: 108B. Mrs M. Mottershead: 2. C. Pettifer (Midland Electricity Board): 15A, 28A. Peter Rogers (Photographic) Ltd: 95A, 114B. Mrs I. Shore: 36B, 117B. B. Sinkinson: 36A, 84. Mrs L. Woollams and Mrs C. Shelley: 63, 110A, 110B, 127B, 128B. Other photographs are from my own collection and postcards from the Lewis family collection.

# Introduction

Over 200 photographs and postcards showing people, places and events in and around Stafford are reproduced in this book. Most are the work of professional photographers. Their names, where they can be identified, and those of postcard publishers are given in brackets after the title of each picture to acknowledge their contribution to our knowledge of the town and its neighbourhood in years gone by.

By the 1850s photography was more than a chemical curiosity. Glass plates with pre-treated surfaces were available and cameras were less cumbersome. Early self-taught photographers often set up in business with little more than a camera and a dark workroom. Photographs were small (60 x 90mm) and sold mounted on heavy card printed with the photographer's name.

In Stafford the earliest photographer was probably S.P. Wood, about whom nothing is known except that he was living in Gaol Square in 1853. In the 1860s he was followed by others, many who failed to establish a profitable business and closed within a year or two.

Only limited photographic work was available in a town the size of Stafford, so photography was usually combined with another business. William Tilley, who set up a business in Vine Street in 1860, combined photography with the sale of window glass and glass shades, and the manufacture of picture frames. His business later moved to Gaolgate Street and, in 1898, his son Harold moved it to Victoria Road. Robert Flamank (junior), born at Colyton in 1822, was the son of a customs and excise officer who was posted to Stafford. Robert worked as an artist at 25 Greengate Street, where he established a photographic studio in 1858. Around 1881 he moved to Birmingham where his son had set up his own studio. It has been said that most of his glass negatives were cleaned off and used as plant pot covers in a Birmingham greenhouse. William Lapworth had a shop in Gaol Square for around ten years. The earliest reference to him as a photographer is in July 1867 when he took a photograph of the choir at St Mary's church and coloured it for presentation to a clergyman who was leaving.

By the late nineteenth century photography had made great technical strides and studios were better equipped. Having your portrait taken had become popular enough for photographers to make a living, providing that they had a flair for business. David Brigham, an art photographer, opened a studio at Castleberg, opposite the grammar school in Newport Road, around 1870. In 1882 the business was bought by David Bordley who built a new studio called Castleberg Studio behind the house. 'Instantaneous photographs of children and animals' and portraits 'enlarged, coloured and printed on porcelain' were offered at 'the finest studio in the Midlands'. Bordley also made wedding photographs fashionable in the town and sold photographs of local views. In 1899 the business was sold to Frederick Stoate who had trained at Mr Falls' studio in London. At the studio he installed 'the latest and most up-to-date electric lighting for night sittings'. In 1908 the Castleberg Studio was leased to John Vandyke and in 1915 it was bought by Paul Weiss who later changed his name to Wise. Wise sold it to Charles Tooth, a Hednesford photographer, in 1928. By this time the studio was becoming out-of-date and it closed in 1935.

The other principal studio in the town developed out of Harold Tilley's Victoria Street premises. These were bought in 1904 by a partnership of Paul Weiss and Charles Fowke. Fowke came from a family who had run a chemist's shop in Market Square since 1803. The new partnership retained Tilley's picture-framing business but also offered amateur photographers a range of equipment, cameras for hire, practical lessons in photography and free use of a dark room. They also supplied local views to several postcard publishers and produced their own photographic postcards of local events.

In 1915 the partnership was dissolved when Paul Weiss left to take over the Castleberg Studio. Charles Fowke joined the forces, first in the experimental tank corps, and later as an air photographer in France. After the war, he returned to Victoria Road where he continued his photographic business and published more postcards of local events. Bertram Sinkinson, a young prize-winning photographer, joined the business in 1934 and took over when Fowke retired in 1938. The studio closed when Sinkinson retired in the 1970s.

Among other professional photographers who have had studios in Stafford, two need to be briefly mentioned because some of their work is included in this book. Albert Guy had a studio in Newport Road from 1912 to around 1939 and took many photographs of local events which he sold as photographic postcards. Thomas Pearce had a small studio in Peel Terrace from 1905 to the 1930s and built up a steady business based on portraits of working men and their families at the north end of Stafford, with a small number of postcards of events that might be of interest to them.

Although not a professional photographer, Dr J.E.C. Peters of Manchester University needs to be mentioned for his photographic survey of some small buildings in Stafford in the 1960s. These photographs are now in the County Museum at Shugborough and some are reproduced in this book.

Picture postcards began to appear in Britain in 1894 but their use was very limited until the early 1900s. The first Stafford postcard dates from 1901 and since then over 1,500 pictures of the town have been published as postcards. Publishers include local shopkeepers like R.W. Dawson, who ran a newsagent's in Bridge Street, and Mrs E. Leigh, a postmistress at Radford, as well as national companies like Boots and W.H. Smith & Son. Other publishers whose postcards are reproduced include Wyndham & Co., Philip Hunt of Manchester, William Shaw of Burslem, Chester Vaughan, William Blake of Longton, Valentine & Sons of Dundee and Raphael Tuck & Sons of London.

The dates assigned to some of the postcards and photographs reproduced are best-guesses based on a study of the pictures and, in the case of postcards, on any postmark date on those which have been used postally.

# One

# A Tour of
# Stafford Town

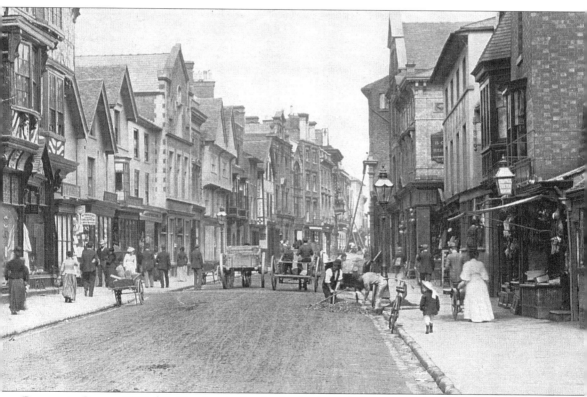

Greengate Street, 1902 (C. Vaughan). At the beginning of the twentieth century the main street of the town had small-paned shop windows and buildings of all ages. Long established local shops such as Averill the chemist, Morgan's wine vaults, Wright & Charrington the printers and stationers, Marson the grocer and Dale the ironmonger dominate the street. In the distance workmen on ladders put up decorative lights outside the Guild Hall in preparation for Edward VII's Coronation celebrations.

Market Square, 1888. Behind the coach and pair is the ornate drinking fountain erected by the Borough Council to mark Queen Victoria's Golden Jubilee in 1887. Opponents of the fountain claimed that it reduced the space for market stalls and also pointed out that the town was still several years away from having a public water supply for the fountain. It was temporarily connected to a tank fed from a well.

Market Square, 1900. The town's weekly markets had been held here since the Middle Ages. When the Guild Hall was built on the west side of the square in 1853, a new covered market was opened behind it, but some traders continued to sell their goods in Market Square. In the foreground is one of the town's horse-drawn cabs waiting to be hired.

Market Square, 1927 (Boots). By the 1920s the increasing number of motor cars was beginning to be a problem in the town. In 1927 the Borough Council removed the remaining stalls from Market Square and laid it out as the town's first car park with underground public toilets discreetly screened by tubs of shrubs.

Market Square, 1927 (Boots). This postcard shows the western side of Market Square. In the centre the building with a projecting balcony is the Guild Hall, which was built in 1853 to house the Borough Council, courts and police. Next to it is Barclays Bank, which was rebuilt in 1924 with a ground floor that projected beyond the upper storeys and provided a grandstand view of any event in the square.

Demolition in Market Square, 1934. The Borough Council decided to make major changes in Market Square in 1934. The Jubilee fountain was pulled down to improve car parking and the Guild Hall knocked down, set back and rebuilt with a shopping arcade. In this photograph Espley & Sons, the local builders, have removed the fountain and begun to demolish the Guild Hall. Note the Woolworth's store to the right of the Guild Hall.

Market Square, 1957 (Boots). On the right the new Guild Hall can be seen with the market entrance flanked by shops. Next to it, the ground floor of Barclays Bank has been set back to the new building line. Further to the left, the ornate three-storeyed front of Boots remains on the old line. In the foreground Market Square has been laid out with gardens and seats to mark the Festival of Britain in 1951.

St John's General Market, 1936. When the Guild Hall was rebuilt, the market behind it was renovated and added to. New stalls were laid out in double lines with wooden frames overhead from which goods could be hung. This photograph and the one below are taken from a booklet published to commemorate the market's improvements.

The Butchers' Market, 1936. In 1880 St John's Market was extended to provide a butchers' market. Since that date a separate butchers' section has always existed. This is the Butchers' Market after the improvements in the 1930s. Note the open tables and the overhead hooks for meat and poultry. William Brown, seen standing behind his stall, was one of a family of butchers who had four shops in the town.

BROOKFIELD'S
STAFFORD.

DRAPERS
& FURNISHER

Brookfield & Windows, 1902. John Boulton is said to have opened a drapery shop in 1743. In 1795 it was transferred to the south side of Market Square. By 1868 it had become Brookfield & Windows and expanded into a second shop. In 1896 four shops on the corner of Market Square and Greengate Street were pulled down to allow Brookfield & Windows to build the town's first department store. Their original shop remained and can be seen on the left of the new building. The arrival of the department store caused as great a revolution in shopping as the more recent opening of supermarkets. For the first time, a lady could buy her dress as well as her hat, gloves and handbag to match in a single shop. In other departments, on different floors, a newly married couple could furnish their whole house. Later, the partnership opened a gentlemen's outfitters in Greengate Street, an ironmongery in Gaolgate Street, their own cabinet making factory in Eastgate Street and a furniture storage and removal business in Foregate.

The corner of Market Square, 1895. This is the corner of Market Square and Greengate Street just before all these premises were demolished to allow Brookfield & Windows to build their department store.

The corner of Market Square, 1924 (Boots). Brookfield & Windows ceased to trade in 1909. A group of senior managers formed Brookfield (Successors) Ltd and carried on the separate shops, but the department store was sold. The Greengate Street premises were converted into two shops and occupied by W.H. Smith & Son and E.F. Allen, a dealer in musical instruments. The part of the building on the corner was bought by Midland Bank who installed new mullioned windows, a corner entrance and a strong room in the cellar.

Coronation day, 1937 (A. Guy). On George VI's Coronation day the 24th Field Battery Royal Artillery, the North Staffordshire Regiment, representatives of the British Legion, firemen, nurses, scouts and guides formed a square in Market Square. The Mayor, councillors and officials walked across in twos and assembled on a red carpeted dais in front of the Shire Hall. A loyal address was read and everyone joined in the National Anthem before parading to the grammar school playing field in Newport Road where a salute was fired.

Hospital Saturday, 1911 (J. Vandyke). Every year a collection in aid of Staffordshire General Infirmary was made in the town. Flowers, pot plants and fruit donated by those with gardens and greenhouses were sold from stalls. Other flowers were made into small bunches and button holes and sold by girls with trays. This is the Mayoress Mrs Westhead's stall in Market Square, with nurses and borough officials as well as helpers.

The High House, 1903 (Wyndham & Co.). The High House, which was built by the Dorringtons in 1595 as their town house, was bought by John Marson in 1826. He had the ground floor converted into three shops. William Marson, born here in 1840, was apprenticed to a London grocer before taking over his father's shop. In 1885 he put in new windows and made his shop 'A High Class grocery establishment and Italian Warehouse'. The shop on the right belonged to W. Wynne the bootmaker and was later taken over by Brookfields.

## ——— YE OLDE CURIOSITIE SHOPPE, ———
### THE ANCIENT HIGH HOUSE, GREENGATE, STAFFORD.

Three minutes' walk from Station.

## W. A. Marson
Proprietor.

FOR SALE:
Antique Furniture,
Glass and China,
Mirrors, Barometers
Clocks, Curios,
Musical Instruments,
Pictures, Prints,
Wedgwood Ware
Milner's Safes,
Oak Chests,
Chippendale Chairs,
Washstands, Bidets,
Bureaus, Cabinets,
Tables, &c., &c.

A visit invited.

Ye Olde Curiositie Shoppe, 1906. Around 1890 William Marson also opened an antique shop in premises behind The High House. He is seen here, with his stock spilling onto the pavement, in an advertisement from A Handbook and Guide to Stafford, published in 1906.

Greengate Street, 1907 (W.H. Smith & Son). The building on the left with two gables and projecting upper floors dates back to the seventeenth century. In 1906 W.H. Smith & Son bought it from Wright and Charrington, printers and stationers. The door on the far side of the shop led upstairs to Smith's wholesale department. Beyond that, the first floor bay windows belong to Charles Morgan & Son's wine vaults, which has now become Waterstone's bookshop with much altered ground floor windows.

Greengate Street, 1910 (R.W. Dawson). The building on the right is said to date from around 1500. It was already an ironmonger's shop when bought by Philip Dale in 1835 and remained in the family for three generations until it was pulled down in the 1950s. A little further along the street are the fishmonger's shop owned by A.W. Green since the 1860s; The Bear Inn rebuilt in 1882; and Briggs' shoe shop which opened in 1909 on the site of The Roebuck Inn.

Greengate Street, 1902 (P. Hunt). The Stafford Bank opened its doors in 1807 but was declared bankrupt in 1830. Its business was taken over by the Manchester & Liverpool District Bank whose first premises are on the extreme left of this postcard. From 1907 to 2007 the premises were occupied by Evans & Evans and are now Countryside Residential Lettings. They are still called Bank house. The bank built itself new premises next door with three gables and a curious mixture of styles. In the 1970s this was replaced by the present National Westminster bank buildings.

The Manchester and Bradford warehouse, Greengate Street, 1908. The warehouse opened at 42 Greengate Street in 1898 and soon afterwards rebuilt the left-hand half of its premises to provide the large display windows seen in this photograph. All manner of domestic linen, curtains and clothes were sold. The Britannia Building Society now occupies this site.

Mill Street, 1927. These three dilapidated cottages are at the Greengate Street end of Mill Street. The premises beyond them were used as a printing works at one time. On the right, the advertisement which reads, 'Smoke Foursome Cigarettes, Bigger and Better' is on the side wall of A. Dobson's tobacconist shop in Greengate Street. All these buildings, except Dobson's shop, have now been pulled down and the new shops built in their place set back to widen the road.

The Swan Hotel stables, Mill Street, 1959. The stables, coach house and harness room on the left were built for The District Bank in the nineteenth century. By the 1950s they were redundant and converted for use by photographer Peter Rogers. After serving at RAF Stafford during the war, Mr Rogers opened his first shop and studio above premises in Greengate Street in 1946. After moving several times he took over these premises in 1959.

Mill Bank, 1928. In 1928 the Borough Council decided to demolish most of the premises of Henry Mercer, the saddler and harness maker, as well as an old building and a roadside wall behind them, in order to widen the road. During the work, the foundations of the medieval town wall were discovered under the more recent wall and stonework from the Green Gate was found under the shop. This photograph was taken just before the work began.

The Royal Brine Baths, 1897. In the 1880s borings at Stafford Common to find a water supply for the town had to be abandoned when a thick bed of salt was discovered. However, the discovery allowed salt water to be pumped to the Royal Brine Baths in Greengate Street which opened in 1892. The Royal Brine Baths provided a swimming pool, Turkish baths and a variety of brine baths that were recommended for those suffering from rheumatism and muscular strains. The price of admission to the pool was sixpence, with an extra twopence for a hot sheet afterwards.

The Royal Brine Baths' boatyard, 1912 (R.W. Dawson). A footpath at the side of the baths led down to this riverside boatyard where rowing boats and canoes could be hired for sixpence from 'Old Joe'. For many years the boating concession was held by Martin Mitchell a town councillor, cycling expert, popular musician and entertainer, and the driving force behind the town's first motor bus service.

The Stafford Volunteer Fire Brigade, 1913. The brigade had a horse-drawn, steam-powered engine named *Elizabeth* which was housed next to The Royal Brine Baths. The open-sided tower of the baths was designed to allow their hoses to be hoisted up and left to dry. In 1913, after criticism of the time taken to turn out a horse-drawn engine, a motorised Leyland pump with a wheeled escape was bought and christened *Catherine*. *Elizabeth* and *Catherine* were photographed together on the grammar school playing field.

The White Bridge, 1915. When the Sow was dredged to allow boats from Radford to bring coal into the town, a short canal was cut to a wharf just short of the Green Bridge. The river is on the right and the canal on the left. The White Bridge allowed men and horses hauling boats to cross the river from the towpath to the wharf. Later, after the canal was filled in, it provided a convenient pedestrian crossing over the river.

Alexandra Hotel, Stafford.

The Alexandra Hotel, 1906. This building on the corner of Tipping Street and Greengate Street was built by Thomas Lovett, a wine merchant, late in the eighteenth century, but its cellars are much older. It was both Lovett's home and his business premises. It became a hotel in 1900 and in 1903 was bought by William Cummins who named it the Alexandra Hotel after Edward VII's Queen. The hotel closed in 1961 and a Superdrug store now occupies the site.

The Picture House, 1914 (W. Shaw). The Picture House, which opened on 23 February 1914, was the foremost cinema in Stafford until the opening of the Odeon in the 1930s. Its tip-up seats rose in tiers before a pit, where soft background music played, and a plush rose-coloured curtain masked the screen. The *Staffordshire Advertiser* described it as 'one of the most up-to-date and luxurious buildings of its kind'.

Bridge Street, 1934 (Valentine & Sons). The Picture House is showing Conrad Veidt in *The Wandering Jew* and on the opposite side of the road F.H. Burgess Ltd has a display of garden furniture in front of their shop. The lamp-post carries a Free Parking Ground sign with a hand pointing down the side of Chicago Rock Café. Lower down the lamp-post, an Even sign is a reminder that waiting in Greengate Street was allowed on one side on even dates and on the other side on odd dates.

Coronation decorations in Bridge Street, 1953. The street decorations in Stafford for the Coronation of Elizabeth II attracted visitors from a wide area. The whole of the main street was 'roofed' with red, white and blue festoons suspended from white poles in blue tubs. At each end of the street an archway carried a banner that read, 'Long Live the Queen'. Every lamp-post was decorated with a basket of geraniums and a cluster of flags held together by a shield. Shops added to the display with flags, garlands and window displays with large pictures of the Queen. Side streets had their own decorations. Particularly striking was Coronation Road where red, white and blue hoops, each decorated with a golden crown, surmounted every gate and flags were suspended from the roofs. In Victoria Park, there were illuminated flower beds and a floral set piece with a waterfall. At night fairy lights outlined the pavilion and a gondola anchored on the Sow. The Stafford Amateur Operatic Society performed *Merrie England* in the park. Fifty street parties for children were planned, although many were driven indoors by the weather. However, New Street spread huge tarpaulins like awnings all down the street and the children's party went on beneath them.

Hill & Halden, printers, 1860s. Victoria Buildings, on the corner of Bridge Street, was built for Hill & Halden in 1850. The stationery and fancy goods department was on the first floor. The ground floor included a shop let to T. Hopkinson. In 1870 the printing business moved to Eastgate Street and the building was converted into The Grapes public house.

Newport Road, 1934. This is the Lichfield Road end of Newport Road. The shops are, from right to left: Clara Ralphs, newsagent; Frederick Avery, confectioner; and Arthur Kenny's fish and chip saloon, to which sacks of potatoes are being delivered from a horse-drawn dray. The cottages beyond the fish and chip saloon are boarded up awaiting demolition. In 1936 the Odeon cinema opened on this site.

The Green, *c.* 1925. A brewery established on the west side of The Green around 1860 was bought by Charles Eley in 1879. Eley's Stafford Brewery expanded steadily. In 1928 the company was taken over by Butler's of Wolverhampton who closed the brewery. The entrance to the brewery yard is on the far left with the offices next to it. The houses on the right include a doctor's surgery. Later F.H. Burgess Ltd, agricultural engineers, acquired the site and pulled down the brewery buildings. Today the Friary Retail Park is here.

The White Lion, Lichfield Road, *c.* 1910. This inn was on the site of the medieval St John's Hospital. The older, west end of the building (on the right) incorporated stone reused from the hospital. Both the inn and White Lion Street were demolished in 1970 when the traffic island at the Lichfield Road end of Queensway was built.

Forebridge Hall, 1914. Charles Webb, a solicitor, built this house in the 1820s on the site of a much older building. Its extensive grounds, including a lodge and drive, stretched along Lichfield Road. The front was built to give the appearance of three storeys but this picture shows that there are no rooms behind the sham windows of the parapet. In 1914 it was occupied by Colonel G. Anson, Chief Constable of Staffordshire. It has now been renamed Green Hall and houses the County Architect's Department.

St Joseph's Convent, 1914 (R.W. Dawson). Forebridge Villa in Lichfield Road was built by the artist and drawing master Benjamin Rogers in the early nineteenth century. Its low-pitched roof and deep eaves are unusual in Stafford. In 1903 the villa was bought by sisters from the French Order of St Joseph of Cluny to establish a convent and girls' school. A large new wing along Lichfield Road was opened in 1932 and now dominates the older building.

Women's Land Army rally, 1919 (C. Fowke). In May 1919 a rally of Women's Land Army members was held in the Shire Hall. One contingent, in working uniform of white smock, wideawake hat and leggings, was photographed in Lichfield Road. Their banners reads, The Nations Food and God Save the King. In the Shire Hall 109 members were presented with good service badges by Lady Gaunt and Mrs Levett, Chairwoman of the Women's War Agricultural Committee, before everyone was served tea in the YWCA.

Lichfield Road, 1920s. These thatched cottages, dating from the seventeenth century, stood in Lichfield Road opposite Forebridge Hall. For many years, one cottage was the home of a chimney sweep. Today they have all been demolished and W.R. Davies' Toyota garage occupies the site. Beyond the cottages, the tall three-storey building was Browse Antiques for many years. In the distance the spire of the Baptist church can be seen.

Lichfield Road, 1902 (C. Vaughan). Charles Webb of Forebridge Hall owned all this land north-west of Lichfield Road. In 1844 he gave part of it as a site for St Paul's church, which is just visible on the right. Later, more land was sold off for 'genteel family residences'. The Oval was laid out in the 1870s and the two houses between the church and The Oval were built around 1890.

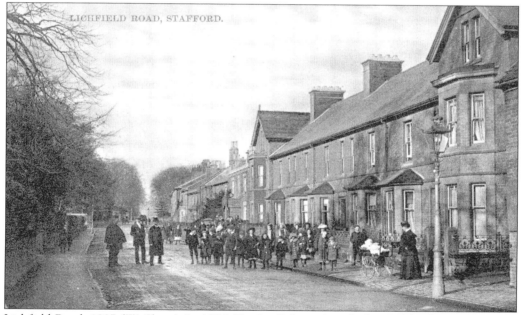

Lichfield Road, 1907 (W. Shaw). In 1886 Charles Calvert described a ramble, 'leaving St Paul's church, we pass through the little suburb of the Hough'. These substantial terraced houses, built in the 1870s, were part of that little suburb. The photographer has persuaded pupils from St Leonard's School as well as a lady with a high pram, two passing men and a police constable to pose for his postcard picture. There was obviously less traffic on Lichfield Road in those days!

Wolverhampton Road, 1905 (W. Shaw). In the distance is the tall four-storeyed Camden Place, built for Richard Ford at the beginning of the nineteenth century. The building was demolished when Queensway was built. The other houses still exist. On the right is Talbot Place, which dates from around 1820. The houses beyond Garden Street (on the right) are now a shop, Gentle Dental Care and a doctor's surgery.

Party at the Telegraph Inn, early 1960s. A small club for senior citizens met regularly at the Telegraph Inn in Wolverhampton Road where Doris Greenwood organized a variety of outings, parties and whist drives. Among those photographed with their balloons at one of the parties are: Mrs Whitworth, Mrs Johnson, Mrs Pontefract and Miss Greenwood who is back row, first right.

Laying ballast, 1890s. This gang with shovels are laying ballast on the Trent Valley railway line near Stafford No. 1 Signal Box. The Wolverhampton Road Bridge over the railway is in the distance on the right and the line to Wolverhampton passes behind the signal box and on the far side of the telegraph pole on the left. The bearded foreman with his bowler hat stands in front of his gang and the two look-out men with their flags are to the left and right.

Burton Manor, 1929. The present red-brick house was built by Francis Whitgreave in 1855, on a site with a moat, where an old house had once stood. During excavations in Foregate a stone cross from the medieval Grey Friars was found and presented to Francis Whitgreave who built it into his house. In 1930 the house was bought by the British Reinforced Concrete Company as a social club for their employees. It became part of Stafford Grammar School in 1982.

Friars Terrace, 1928. These three cast-iron bollards separated Telegraph Street and the southern end of Friars Terrace, which were wide enough for cars and carts to use, from the rest of Friars Terrace and Friars Road, which were much narrower. On the left is the factory of Heels Ltd, once the largest maker of wooden heels in the country, and on the right is the police barracks.

Friars Road, 1928. In the centre are Jubilee Cottages with Friars Walk behind them. On the left, the new wing of King Edward VI Grammar School is nearing completion, although the scaffolding can still be seen and the roof of the hall is no more than a wooden skeleton. As soon as the building was completed, the wall in front of it was knocked down and the road widened.

Tennis club, Friars Terrace, 1926. This tennis club, with courts next to the factory of Heels Ltd, flourished in the 1920s. The players posed in this group include: Mr Swynnerton, Bert Yates and Jim Norton in the front row. In the background Park Street and the police barracks can be seen. The site is now a car park.

Park Street from Wolverhampton Road, 1905 (W. Blake). The first police barracks were at the back of the Guild Hall. When these were demolished in 1867, in order to extend the covered market, new barracks were built on the corner of Austin Friars and Friars Terrace. In 1882 the larger militia barracks, seen on the left, became vacant and the police moved into them. The County Library building is now on the site. The sign on the opposite corner belongs to The Britannia public house, whose licensee was Richard Hopper.

The Bloor family, c. 1905. David and Elizabeth Bloor sit in the garden of their home at Brooklands with some of their eleven children. George Bloor (front row, first left) was the manager of a salt manufactory and married Rosa Webb (back row, centre). The photograph appears to have been taken on some sort of musical occasion.

C.E. Fowke, 1951 (B. Sinkinson). C.E. Fowke was, for many years, the leading photographer in Stafford (see introduction). After he retired from business in 1938, he began a second career as a member of the Borough Council. He became an alderman in 1948 and was Mayor from 1951 to 1953. He retired from the council in 1955 and died at his home in Rising Brook in 1965, aged eighty-nine.

Rowley Hall, 1867 (R. Flamank). William Keen, a Stafford solicitor, bought the Rowley estate in 1811. He built this house in place of the dilapidated building on the site and landscaped the grounds around it. In 1828 he was severely kicked by a horse in his stable yard and died. The Hall was later sold to The Staffordshire Land, Building and Improvement Company who developed part of the estate for housing. Today, the Hall is a private hospital.

The hall, Rowley Hall, 1928. The hall was photographed just before Rowley Hall was sold by Mrs Dobell to the County Home for Discharged Female Prisoners, which later became a Home Office Remand Home. One of the girls sent there recalled that her first job each morning was to clean this ornate staircase before breakfast. If the job was not completed properly before 8.00 a.m. she had no breakfast. The school closed in 1981.

The maids at Rotherwood, 1908. Nicholas Joyce was an architect who set up a business in Stafford in 1869. In 1887 he bought land at the back of Westhorpe in Rowley Avenue where he built a large house called Rotherwood. In 1900 Joyce sold his practice to H. Sandy and retired. The maids were photographed in uniform outside the front door of the drawing room. In the 1990s the house was pulled down and Maple Court Nursing Home built on the site.

The coachman, Rotherwood, 1908. Cornelius Harrod, Nicholas Joyce's coachman and groom at Rotherwood, is standing outside the front door. The house had a lodge in Hargreaves Lane where the coachman lived with his family. Nicholas Joyce died in 1908 but Cornelius Harrod continued in his widow's service until he moved to Manchester around 1915.

Westhorpe, 1920s. W.H. Peach, a shoe manufacturer living at Friars Cottage in Friars Terrace, moved into this newly built house in Rowley Avenue around 1897. By the 1920s the owner was Richard Young. Later it became a County Council Home for the elderly and many additions were made to it. The home closed in 2004.

Stafford station, 1927. By the 1860s the number of passengers and trains at Stafford had increased so much that a new and larger station was needed. The building shown here was opened in 1862 and four years later the Station Hotel was built opposite the entrance to provide quality accommodation for visitors arriving by train. The station survived almost unchanged in outward appearance until it was pulled down in the 1960s. The hotel was demolished in 1972.

Locomotives at Stafford, 1892. Two Problem Class locomotives stand at the southern end of the station. No. 229, *Watt*, with its tender stacked with coal, has just backed onto a train of coaches and a horsebox is being coupled between the tender and coaches. At this time, ashes were still spread over the track to cover the sleepers and hide any defects. The central pole on the up fast line supported a signal known as *Big Ben*, which survived until the 1950s.

Stafford station, 1950s. The 1862 station had only two platforms for through trains, with bays at the end of each for local trains. Goods lines were at the back of the platforms. Platform three was added in 1880 and others followed later. Note the water column at the end of platform one. In the 1960s the whole station was remodelled with a new bridge connecting the platforms.

*Isabel* removed, 1978. This narrow gauge saddle-tank locomotive was built at Stafford by W.G. Bagnall Ltd in 1897 for the Cliffe Hill Granite Company. In 1952 she returned to Stafford and, after being rebuilt by Bagnall apprentices, was displayed at the works and later opposite the railway station. *Isabel* gradually deteriorated and in 1978 was removed for repair. She was restored by the Staffordshire Narrow Gauge Railway Society and is now at Amerton Farm.

Izaak Walton Walk, 1903 (Wyndham & Co.). The walk along the river bank was decked out with seats and iron railings in 1880 as part of a river improvement scheme undertaken by the Borough Council, after they bought the town mill. In the early 1900s trees were planted along the length of Izaak Walton Walk to make it more attractive. The Victoria Road bridge and Station Hotel can be seen in the background.

Victoria Pleasure Gardens, 1908. The land between Izaak Walton Walk and the station was marshy. In 1903 the council began raising the level by three feet in order to convert the land into pleasure gardens. Work proceeded slowly, but by 1908 four acres had been planted and the bandstand from Market Square re-erected in the gardens. There was no official opening. This photograph was taken a few days after the gates were opened on 15 June 1908. A month later came the first reports of vandalism and litter bins were also provided urgently.

Opening the extension to Victoria Park, 1911. To mark the Coronation of King George V, Victoria Park was extended across the river towards Tenterbanks, and the Coronation Bridge was built to link the two parts. The extension included a bowling green. On the afternoon of Coronation Day the Mayoress, Mrs Westhead, ceremonially unlocked the gate in Victoria Road with a silver key before inspecting the gardens and watching a short bowls match.

Broadeye Mill from the park, 1950s. Victoria Park was extended further across Victoria Road in 1930. The extension provided tennis courts, a children's playground and a paddling pool. This photograph, taken from across the river, shows the extension with Broadeye Mill in the background. The machinery had been removed in the 1890s and the premises were then used by James Marsh, a mineral water manufacturer. By the 1930s it was derelict and remained in that state until the 1990s.

A new bridge over the Sow, 1933. When Victoria Road and bridge were constructed in the 1860s as a new approach to the railway station, the soft ground by the river was an engineer's nightmare. The first brick bridge collapsed almost as soon as it was built and William Moss was called in to rebuild it with steel girders on heavily piled supports. His bridge lasted until 1933. The same problem of soft ground was faced by the builders of the new bridge. Some piles went down eighty feet without reaching solid ground.

The old Victoria Road Bridge, 1933. The old bridge has been partly demolished and a crane erected on the South Street side of the river is lifting the old steel girders, which had become badly corroded. In the background Tenterbanks School can be seen.

Victoria Road Bridge, 1933 (E. Loveys). The new bridge, built in 1933, was designed by William Plant, the Borough Surveyor and Engineer, with a single sixty-six feet span of reinforced concrete. Eric Loveys took this photograph while the wooden frame for supporting the shuttering of the reinforced concrete was being assembled.

Tenterbanks from Victoria Road, 1929 (C. Fowke). All of these buildings have been demolished. In 1929, beyond the early nineteenth-century terraced houses on the right, was Tenterbanks School, and in the distance is the chimney of Broadeye Mill. The chimney had been added and an engine house built at the back when the mill was converted to steam power. In 1930, when the park was extended, the wall and buildings on the left were pulled down to widen the road.

Tenterbanks from Broadeye, 1929 (C. Fowke). This is the view seen when standing outside Broadeye Mill and looking towards Victoria Road. The buildings on the left were pulled down when the College of Further Education was built. The early nineteenth-century houses on the right were taken down soon after this photograph was taken. The photographer, Charles Fowke, has attracted the attention of those who lived in the houses as well as that of a resident black cat and a dog.

The Town Mill, 1918 (H.O. Jones). The medieval town mill was rebuilt by George Brewster in 1834. It was powered by two undershot wheels fed from the mill pool by a culvert under the roadway in the foreground. The mill ceased to work in 1957 and has now been demolished. The site has been converted into an extension to Victoria Park with the waterwheels left in position. The drawing is by H.O. Jones, the son of George Jones of the Crescent Pottery, Stoke-on-Trent, who used to live at Newport House in Stafford.

The Horse and Jockey, 1905. This public house was on the corner of Water Street and Tenterbanks. In 1905 the licensee was Harry Scott, whose family and pet dog are pictured outside the public house. The name Horse and Jockey may seem out of place in Stafford but in the mid-nineteenth century, when it was opened, there were racing stables at Deanshill on Newport Road and occasional race meetings held on Stafford Common.

Water Street from Mill Bank, 1938 (A. Guy). The Horse and Jockey on the left has been turned into a shop. The houses on the opposite corner were pulled down shortly after this photograph was taken and in 1942 a temporary fire station was built here, replacing the old fire station by The Royal Brine Baths. The temporary station was in use until a new fire station was built at Lammascote in 1969.

The Noah's Ark, Crabbery Street, 1920. Queen Elizabeth is said to have taken wine here during a visit to the town. There is no proof that she did, but much of the building is certainly old enough. In the 1880s it was bought by the Borough Council who took down the half-timbered entrance porch and rebuilt the right-hand end of the building to widen the street. The curved corner wall of reused stone dates from this time. In 1967 the building was converted into the market's office.

Bath Street, 1923. This was once the home of Colonel William Brookes, a retired East India Company officer, who had an illegitimate daughter called Anne by his housekeeper. When Anne grew up she married William Palmer, the notorious Rugeley poisoner. Both Anne and her mother were among Palmer's victims. In 1923 the premises were occupied by Scott & Clarke the drapers. On the left is the smithy of Samuel Davis, a registered shoeing smith.

Police station, Bath Street, 1970s. In the late nineteenth century the police station was on the ground floor of the Guild Hall in Market Square. It became too cramped and in 1931 this new police station was built on the corner of Bath Street, the site of Scott & Clarke's drapers shop. The premises were boarded up after the police station was transferred to Eastgate Street.

Fire in Gaolgate, 1887 (D. Bordley). On 1 October 1887 the large half-timbered Elizabethan House in Gaolgate Street caught fire. The volunteer fire brigade turned out with its manual pumps but the jets of water could not reach the top of the building. The fire spread and destroyed the old Maid's Head Inn and Mummery's jewellery and watch shop on the corner of Market Square, as well as the Elizabethan House itself. David Bordley photographed the scene the next day, after clearing up had begun. Immediately afterwards, the council raised money for a more powerful steam fire engine. The 1905 William Shaw postcard below shows the same corner of Market Square after it had bean rebuilt.

GAOLGATE STREET, STAFFORD.

The Dolphin Hotel, 1910. The Dolphin was in Gaolgate Street opposite Salter Street. The original seventeenth-century half-timbered building, sold by George Craddock in 1642, had upper floors that overhung the street. In the eighteenth century it was given a new front. The doorway on the left led along a passage to a narrow yard with stables at the end and a market room on the right. On the first floor the dining room looked out over the street and other rooms spread over the adjoining shop.

Gaolgate Street looking north, 1903 (C. Vaughan). On the left is Henry Cliff's tea and coffee warehouse which was established in 1794 and advertised itself as 'the oldest tea shop in the district'. Next door, Joseph Richardson sold glass, earthenware, furniture and ironmongery. On the opposite side of the road, the Shaving Rooms sign belongs to Batkin & Kent, hairdressers and athletic outfitters, and a little further along the road is Samuel Lovell's English Cheese Warehouse which sold bacon, ham and butter as well as cheese.

Gaolgate Street looking south, 1914 (Royal Baths' Tobacco Shop). On the right are the London Central Meat Co. and the double brick gable of The Maypole Dairy Company, the forerunners of national companies opening branches in the town. Part of the building beyond them is the Edward VII public house which changed its name from the Bricklayers' Arms to mark the King's Coronation. On the opposite side of the road is the shop of T.B. Maylott, a pastry cook, with a high basketwork baby carriage outside.

Thorn & Co., 1962 (M. Peters). Thorn & Co. had premises in Gaolgate Street which stretched back along Salter Street, where there was a rear entrance to a large yard. The company, established in 1743, was described in 1903 as ironmongers, gas fitters, locksmiths, bell hangers and tinsmiths. The old tinplating works can be seen in this photograph of the yard.

H.R. Weaver, 1930. Henry Richard Weaver had a nursery in Garden Street and a small florist's shop at 2 Salter Street. His son, also Henry Richard, became an electrical contractor and opened this shop further along Salter Street at No. 15 in 1929. In the window are electric light shades and fittings, fires and an electric iron.

Sidney Fountain and Sidney House, 1904 (Valentine & Sons). Thomas Sidney was born in the house on the left, later known as Sidney House. He was MP for the town and later Lord Mayor of London. In 1889, shortly after his death, his widow had this drinking fountain erected in Gaol Square in his memory. The fountain originally had a statue of Sampson above a pair of lamps but, when electric street lights were erected in Gaolgate Street, the statue was replaced by a third lamp on a lengthened standard.

Sidney Fountain destroyed, 1928. In May 1928 a motor van backed into the fountain and toppled the whole structure. Fortunately, water had been cut off some years before due to concern about hygiene. The fountain was replaced by a clock on a pillar. In the background, the building in North Walls with semicircular headed windows housed King Edward VI Grammar School from 1813 to 1862.

Gaol Square, 1905 (W. Shaw). The Union Jack boot and shoe store, 'the working man's friend', is prominent in the centre. To the right is one of three cast-iron 'conveniences for gentlemen' put up by the Borough Council and in the distance is the Primitive Methodist Chapel (see p. 92). On the left is Foregate Street and Hoyle's picture framing shop with its sunblinds down. The tower of Christ Church can just be seen over the other buildings.

GAOL SQUARE, STAFFORD.

Gaol Square, 1927 (Excel). In the centre, the Sidney Fountain has had its third lamp replaced by a four-dial clock presented by George Bruckshaw of Tillington to mark his fifty years residence in Stafford. Gaol Square Garage, opened by H.K. Hales in 1907, had been relaunched in 1911 under new management with John Bagnall as manager and advertised, 'cars painted, lined and varnished; driving tuition a speciality'. The Methodist New Connection Chapel is to the right of the Sidney Fountain.

Gaol Square Improvement Scheme, 1931. By 1930 Gaol Square was becoming a traffic hazard. Several accidents, including the destruction of the Sidney Fountain, had occurred there. The Borough Council, therefore, decided to carry out a traffic improvement scheme. A new clock on a concrete pillar was erected some yards from where the Sidney Fountain had stood and one end of the Gaol Square Garage was pulled down to widen the road. Note the roadside petrol pumps with a different top for each company.

Gaol Square, 1953 (R. Tuck & Sons). This is the west side of the square with the Elephant and Castle public house on the right. Next to it is Lake's Dairy. In the 1930s this was started by Mrs Lake and her sister-in-law. They had a popular line in home-made cakes and were the first shop in town to sell cooked meats. There were no cooking facilities at the shop so a kitchen was hired behind Frape's gentlemen's hairdressing salon (on the left) and cakes, joints of meat and roast chickens were carried across Mount Street on tin trays covered with grease proof paper.

Foregate Street looking north, 1927 (W. Shaw). On the left, the Staffordshire General Infirmary lies behind the high wall and shrubbery put there in 1896 to add privacy to the premises. On the right is a row of early nineteenth-century houses including The Plume of Feathers public house with its oval hanging sign. The public house is first mentioned in 1834. In recent years road widening has resulted in the setting back of the infirmary wall and the demolition of most of the houses on the right.

Babies' ward, Staffordshire General Infirmary, c. 1910. All the wards were upgraded in 1897 when extensive alterations and additions were made to the infirmary. This ward for the youngest children is decorated for Christmas with a magnificent tree and presents donated by townspeople piled around it.

County Road, 1915. Both The Greyhound in the distance and The King's Head in the foreground have been here since the early nineteenth century. The houses on the right were built a little later. This view is still easily recognisable although The King's Head is now Al Sheikh's Balti Restaurant and the wall on the left has been knocked down to provide a car park for the William Sutton Trust.

Foregate Street looking south, 1906 (W. Shaw). The photographer must have stood in the middle of the street, near its junction with Browning Street, to take this picture. On the left, behind the wall, is Dorman's original factory and on the right is the entrance to Snow's Yard. The paper boy on the pavement on the left and other children from nearby houses have all stopped to stare at the photographer.

The Forehead, 1915. The road from Stafford to Stone and Eccleshall divided at The Forehead, a local name in use since the seventeenth century. At the place where the roads diverged was The Waggon and Horses, a rear view of which is on the right. In 1827 Robert Adams had a ninety-nine year lease of the premises but there was an inn here before that. Today the roads divide further north where a traffic roundabout has been constructed. The length of the Stone road seen in the foreground is now a backwater.

The bar of The Waggon and Horses, 1930s. The bar has been decorated for Christmas and the wine list is pinned up over it. The licensee in the 1930s was Thomas Puzey, who moved here from The Dolphin before the First World War.

The Waggon and Horses, 1905. At the back of the premises was a small brewery. In the late nineteenth century this was re-equipped and extended by William Greatrex as The Foregate Brewery, which supplied ale in casks to private houses as well as a few other public houses. When Greatrex died in 1911 the public house was said to have, 'a wide reputation for its home brewed ales', and as a result, 'does an exceptionally large business'. The premises have been altered and extended since Greatrex's day.

Horsley Bros, 1914. Horsley Bros, house furnishers and removal contractors, first appeared in the *Stafford Directory* for 1905 when they were based at 9 Common Road. By 1914, after several moves, they were based at 95 Marston Road where this photograph was taken. The horses are dressed with plumes and horse brasses, and the van wheels decorated either in the traditional May Day style of those who worked with horses or for the hospital pageant. Horsley's is still a family business andnow has premises on Tollgate Park

Sandon Road, 1914 (N. Norris). This postcard was published by Nellie Norris who kept a shop at 44 Gaol Road where she sold toys, stationery, newspapers, useful and fancy articles, and postcards. Advertisements describe it as, 'the noted shop for picture postcards'. Sometimes postcards remained in stock for several years. This one, published in 1914, was bought by Mrs Rothery in June 1925 and sent to a friend saying that she was staying at 101 Sandon Road (marked with a cross) a little longer 'because it is so nice here'.

Coton Field allotments, 1916. Many working men took great pride in their allotments. In 1916 William Conniff (senior) was presented by the Mayoress with a medal for the best decorated allotment hut. The interior walls were covered with carefully arranged colourful pictures of fruit and flowers. Two comfortably cushioned chairs were drawn up to a table covered with a fringed cloth on which were vases for flowers. Tools were all spotlessly clean. William is seen here with his son William (junior) and his wife.

The towers of the gaol, 1951. In the mid-nineteenth century a tower was added at each corner of the gaol to provide living quarters for warders and vantage points to watch the walls. When the gaol was enlarged in 1865, the north-west tower in Crooked Bridge Road was taken down and rebuilt next to the one on the corner of Gaol Road. This pair of towers remained until demolished for road improvements in 1953.

Council houses in the gaol, 1921. The gaol was disused from 1920 to 1939. During the housing shortage of the 1920s the warders' quarters were taken over by the Borough Council. An old inhabitant recalls, 'When I was a child we lived in a tower of Stafford Gaol that was rented to us as a council house. It was all round – the rooms were round and the staircase spiral. The rent was 9 shillings and 9 pence a week.'

The gate-lodge, 1952 (R. Clegg). The original gate-lodge of the gaol projected out from the high boundary wall and a second lower wall ran level with its front. The flat roof provided a platform for public executions until 1817, when the scaffold collapsed during the execution of Anne Statham for the murder of her daughter. After that, a scaffold on wheels was pushed out through the gateway. In 1952, in order to widen Gaol Road, the second low wall and the gate-lodge were pulled down after a new gate and gate-lodge had been built by the prisoners.

Female prisoners at exercise, 1868 (R. Flamank). In the 1840s a new system of prison discipline was introduced. Prisoners were to be kept apart as much as possible and forbidden to speak to each other so that the innocent minded would not be contaminated by the depraved. A new female prison was opened in 1852 to allow this to be introduced at Stafford Gaol. These women are at silent exercise, watched over by a wardress in her sentry box. Note the prisoner far right with a child in her arms.

Inside the female prison, 1868 (R. Flamank). The pictures on this page and the next are from a series of photographs that Robert Flamank took of the interior of Stafford Gaol in 1868. The interior of the women's prison is seen from the third landing, with tiers of cells on either side and a central space open to the roof to allow better supervision.

The reception ward, 1868 (R. Flamank). New prisoners lined up under the eye of a warder who appears to be checking their names against a list. The chaplain waits by the wall in the background.

Debtors, 1868 (R. Flamank). Those who failed to repay a debt might have been imprisoned until the money was paid. Prisoners for debt were always allowed privileges if they could pay for them. Hot dinners could be sent in from The Greyhound opposite the gaol, and a prisoner could wear his own clothes. These are County Court debtors who had a room where they could sit and read or talk at specified times. At other times they were compelled to sit or stand in the exercise yard.

Market Street, 1920. All these shops were pulled down in the 1960s. The building with a car parked in front was a tea warehouse in the late eighteenth century, when tea was still an expensive luxury from China. Four large oriental figures sat on the parapet overlooking the street as an advertisement. In 1963, when the shop was demolished, the figures were moved to a museum on the first floor of the library building at The Green and are now in the County Museum at Shugborough. They are made from very hard plaster known as Roman cement and are very heavy. The photograph below shows how much they are in need of restoration.

Eastgate Street, *c.* 1880 (D. Brigham). The Borough Hall (now The Gatehouse) was opened in 1877, but within a few years part of the gable wall collapsed, damaging the roofs of nearby houses. On the far left is Eastgate House, dating from 1683, but with an eighteenth-century brick frontage. Between the Borough Hall and Eastgate House the sign for The Goat Inn can be seen. Note the curious effect of movement on a timed exposure, which has made part of a horse and cart invisible.

Eastgate Street, 1964 (M. Peters). This is a later view than the one at the top of this page. On the right, the Borough Hall was extended in 1881 to provide space for a library, the Wragge Museum and the School of Art. The line where the gable wall was rebuilt is still clearly visible. Eastgate House and The Goat Inn were both bought by the County Council in 1891. Eastgate House was retained as the residence of the Chief Constable but The Goat Inn was demolished to allow a house for the Superintendent of Police to be built. The police moved out of both buildings in 1961.

Eastgate Street, 1905. This street always had a large number of public houses. In 1835 the first map of Stafford to name public houses shows the Lord Nelson, with the oddly named Cow and Hare opposite it, and The Unicorn at the east end of the street. At the west end are The Castle, The Goat (see p. 69) and the three inns shown here: The White Hart, the three-storeyed Sheridan (now The Forester and Firkin) and the black and white gabled Fox and George.

Martin Street, 1928. On the far right is the ornate frontage of Zion Chapel (see p. 91) and on the left is the Lyceum Theatre with a railed balcony. The theatre was built in 1793, but had fallen into such a poor state of repair by 1912 that it was forced to close. Mrs Thomas refurbished the theatre and renamed it The Playhouse, but in June 1915 the interior was destroyed by fire. The shell of the building was then used as a warehouse by Brookfields until the premises were bought by the County Council and pulled down in 1931.

Martin Street, 1880. This narrow medieval street was known as Smokey Lane in the eighteenth century. In the distance on the left are The Fountain and The Old Blue Posts, two public houses separated by Parker's pork shop, and in the foreground is the Lyceum Theatre. In 1891 all the property on the right was bought by the newly formed County Council to build 'good businesslike offices for county work' at the back of the Shire Hall.

Martin Street, 1895. The County Council held a competition for the design of the new County Buildings. The winner was a young architect called H.T. Hare. Part of his building can be seen on the right. Unfortunately, the County Council had failed to buy the block of offices on the corner of St Martin's Place (in the centre of this picture) and Hare had to design his building around it. In 1897 the County Council bought the office block and Hare designed an extension to the County Buildings.

**OLD BLUE POSTS HOTEL, Stafford.**

**Proprietor—JACK HARVEY.**

English A.A.A. Champion (5 miles) 1910.   Mid. N.C.U. Champion (25 miles) 1909
English A.A.A.      ,,      (1 mile) 1910.   English N.C.U.   ,,      (25 miles) 1909
Northern A.A.A.    ,,      (½ mile) 1910.   Mid. N.C.U.      ,,      (¼ mile) 1908
                   Northern A.A.A. Champion (5 miles) 1910.

The Old Blue Posts, 1889. This public house in Martin Street was close to the Lyceum Theatre and much used by performers there. Harry and Mary Thompson, licensees at the turn of the century, had previously been music hall artistes. With the decline of the theatre, trade at The Old Blue Posts also waned. William Bird, who had been a coachbuilder in Gaol Road, sold his business and borrowed money to take over the public house, paying a rent of £60 a year. In 1905 his takings fell to £9 a week and he was forced to give up The Old Blue Posts and declare himself bankrupt.

Jack Harvey, 1911. A few years after Bird became bankrupt, Eley's brewery tried to attract more custom by giving the lease to Jack Harvey, a well-known Midlands cyclist. This postcard advertised the new proprietor and listed some of his achievements. He remained at The Old Blue Posts until 1915.

# Two

# Around Stafford

High Street, Gnosall, 1905. On the left, the horse and trap are standing outside Samuel Addison's grocery store, which was also an agency for Gilbey's wines and spirits. On the right is George Sidebotham's drapery shop.

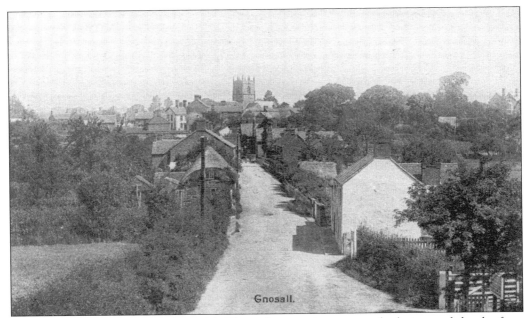

Station Road, Gnosall, 1902 (F. Frith). The railway station was reached via a path by the five-barred gate in the foreground. The station was raised on an embankment so that the line could cross the road by a girder bridge, which provided the photographer with an elevated viewpoint from which to take this picture. The house on the right, beyond the station approach, belonged to Stephen Bernard, a well-known local plumber and decorator.

Gnosall station, 1910. This view is taken from the up platform looking towards Stafford. The garden was a feature of the station and in the distance a porter can be seen at work in it. This line from Stafford to Wellington and Shrewsbury opened in 1849 with three trains each way on weekdays. By 1910 there was also a daily train from London to Aberystwyth via Gnosall.

Gnosall in winter, 1907. The road to Stafford takes a sharp turn to the right by the man with the wheelbarrow. On the left is the old lock-up. This ten feet square room of large stone blocks was built by the parish in 1830 as 'a proper place for the confinement of criminals'.

Coton, Gnosall, 1909 (Perfection series). To take this picture the photographer stood outside Sheaff & Kemp's stores and bakery, looking towards Gnosall. Mill Lane is on the right. The large stone, on which three girls are posed, stopped the wheels of carts turning into the lane from scraping the corner of the house where Sam Plant the local chimney sweep lived. In the distance is William Leese's butchers shop.

Haughton Old Hall, 1914 (W.H. Smith & Son). This half-timbered house was probably built in the time of Elizabeth I. It was restored in 1889 when it belonged to Charles Royds, the rector of Heysham, but has remained substantially unaltered. Its plan is T-shaped with the upright part of the 'T' close studded and probably older than the rest of the building, which has more decorative timber framing. Inside, there are massive beams and fireplaces with stone jambs.

Haughton Football Club, 1913. Unfortunately, nothing is known about this village team who posed with their coach and trainer at the end of the 1912/13 season.

Doxey, 1911 (W.H. Smith & Son). The land where these houses were built came on the market in 1898 when Evans & Evans, the Stafford estate agents, advertised plots at £300 an acre to those intending to build cottage property. They said, 'This is a rare opportunity for railway servants, the land being within a few minutes walk of the engine sheds.' A load of coal has been delivered to one of the houses on the left, but the occupier has not yet moved it into his coal shed.

Hyde Lea school, 1908. The school was built in 1863 to take sixty pupils. The original building remained in use, with little alteration, until the school closed in the 1970s. Today it is the village hall and plans for modernization are well in hand. This postcard was sent by Willie Ward, a pupil who has marked himself with an X, to his cousin Eli Glover in Narberth.

The old smithy, Coppenhall, 1935 (Lilywhite Ltd). The smithy was built between Hyde Lea and Coppenhall, not far from the village school whose proximity is shown by the torch road sign. The first blacksmith to occupy the site was probably William Simcox who was there in the 1840s. He was followed by his son John and in the early 1870s by Benjamin Fletcher. George Fletcher was the smith at the time of this postcard and was still there in the late 1940s.

The Smithy, Sandon, 1907 (W. Shaw). The brothers John and William Cheadle were blacksmiths and wheelwrights here in 1834. In 1907 the smith was Roger Downing who is standing in the doorway, smoking his pipe and resting one hand on a wheel ready to be fitted with its iron tyre. Nearby is farm machinery awaiting repair.

The Dog and Doublet, Sandon, 1905 (W. Shaw). This was a coaching inn in the eighteenth century when stagecoaches from London to Liverpool stopped here to change horses. In the second half of the nineteenth century, when railways replaced horse-drawn coaches, the inn's trade declined. It was rebuilt in 1905, and the adjoining village institute also dates from that year. The workmen in this picture are probably working on the institute rather than the inn.

Tinkerborough, 1906 (Palatine Pictorial Co.). At the top of Weston Bank, turn into Brickiln Lane and take one of the footpaths to Salt. Slew Covert is on the right and David's Rock Covert, with its forgotten cave, on the left. In the narrow gap between the two coverts was Tinkerborough. The few cottages, backing onto the rock, housed workers from the quarry at the top of Weston Bank. It was once a favourite walk and one rambler described it as 'a most romantic and fairy-like spot with rock-hewn cottages and truly beautiful diversity of wood and dell'.

Hillcrest, Weeping Cross, 1914. This house was occupied by Charles Wilton, Deputy Superintendent Registrar and Inquiry Officer for Stafford Poor Law Union. He and his family are relaxing in their garden with a fashionable thatched summer house in the background. In one hand he has his pipe and in the other the dog's lead. His wife has her needlework box open on the table.

Barnfields, 1950s. This late eighteenth-century farmhouse was built by John Twigg. The entrance on the north side had a pillared porch and behind the house lay a range of farm buildings. Some of these incorporated old stonework which is said to have been removed from Baswich church when it was rebuilt. The farmhouse was pulled down when the Kwik Save supermarket was built in the 1970s. The name Barnfields is still preserved in the name of the nearby primary school.

The post office, Walton-on-the-Hill, 1907 (W. Shaw). In 1900 the Woods, from the post office at the Springs, moved into one of these thatched cottages. The post office moved too. Mrs Katherine Woods was postmistress here until the Second World War. Her husband, Samuel, had his own painting and decorating business at the back of the premises. Beyond the post office was the brick and tile smithy where Thomas Fletcher was both blacksmith and keeper of the village pound on the opposite side of the road.

Pool Lane, Brocton, 1907 (W. Shaw). The left-hand side of the road from Milford to Brocton was open to the Chase until this point, where houses began on both sides of the road, and a gate prevented animals from the Chase straying into the village. By 1907 the gate was disused and off its hinges. Today, all that remains is the stump of a gatepost on the grass verge. The house on the right still stands but the one on the left has been pulled down.

Weston-on-Trent, 1908 (A. McCann). Both of these photographs are part of a series taken by Alfred McCann, a Uttoxeter photographer, in 1908. The one above shows The Green, a scene that has changed little over the last ninety years, although The Green is now much better maintained and regularly mown by the parish council. The one below shows the village school, which was built in 1871 on a site given by Earl Ferrers and paid for by Miss Moore of Wychdon at Hixon. In 1908 the schoolmaster was Robert Maundsley and the average attendance ninety-two boys and girls.

# *Three*

# Churches and Schools

Laying the foundation stone of the Men's Institute, St Thomas', Stafford, 1908 (Weiss &
Fowke). St Thomas' church was built in 1866 for railway workers and other residents of the
new suburb of Castletown, Stafford. In 1908 the vicar was Revd W.S. Allen, who is seen here
conducting a special service to mark the laying of the foundation stone of the Men's Institute
next to the church. The building was erected by voluntary labour. Members of the congregation
with building skills brought their tools and worked in the evening. Pictures like this one were
taken and sold as postcards to help raise the £150 needed for the Institute.

St Mary's, Stafford, 1960 (B. Sinkinson). In the Middle Ages the building had almost been two churches: the nave was the parish church and the chancel was used by the dean and canons of the College of St Mary. The dean and canons' were abolished in the sixteenth century and the screen between the two parts of the church removed in the 1840s. This left the congregation remote from the high altar, as this picture shows. In 1963 a new altar was installed under the tower at the end of the nave so that the priest and people were brought closer together during services.

St Chad's, Stafford, 1903 (Wyndham & Co.). This church became so ruinous in the eighteenth century that the west end collapsed. The west end was rebuilt in brick and the rest of the building was cased in brick. At that time there was a row of houses in front of the church, which was reached by a tunnel-like entry between the houses. In the second half of the nineteenth century, the brick was removed, the west end completely rebuilt in Norman style (as seen here) and the houses in front of the church pulled down to open out access to it.

St Lawrence's, Gnosall, 1910 (F. Mears). This is a magnificent building of many periods. The core is a Norman church whose massive pillars support a fifteenth-century tower. The arches under the tower are carved with bands of typical Norman decoration. Behind the altar is a fine fourteenth-century window which was re-glazed after the First World War in memory of the men of the parish who lost their lives.

St Mary's, Castlechurch, 1907. Originally this was a Norman church but the tower was rebuilt to commemorate the marriage of Humphrey Stafford (later Duke of Buckingham) to Margaret Neville in 1424. By 1844 the building was in such a poor state that all of it, except the tower, was knocked down and rebuilt. George Keen of Rowley Hall and his son-in-law, Robert Hand, paid most of the cost. This picture was taken during the exceptionally severe winter of 1906-07.

St Augustine's, Broadeye, 1963 (M. Peters). A school attached to St Mary's, Stafford, was opened at the corner of Duke Street in 1868. Ten years later it was extended by building this mission church next to it. The body of the church was also used as a classroom on weekdays. The church was replaced by St Bertelin's in 1900 and the school closed in 1911. In the 1950s the building was used by the Universal Grinding Wheel Co. as a stationery store and printing department. It was knocked down soon after this picture was taken.

St Bertelin's, Broadeye, 1963 (M. Peters). This church, which replaced St Augustine's, was consecrated in 1900. Its congregation was always poor and few in number but the church ran very active clubs for both boys and girls. The clubs shut down during the First World War and the church itself closed in 1920, although it continued to be used as a Sunday school for another twenty years. It was demolished in 1964 and its foundation stone taken to Holmcroft.

Dedication of St Bertelin's, Holmcroft, 1956. A new church for the growing population of Holmcroft and Tillington was suggested in 1935 and the money from the sale of St Bertelin's at Broadeye was put in a trust for this purpose. Active collecting was renewed after the Second World War and in 1954 F.W. Carder of Tillington Hall offered a site and £1,000 towards the cost. The first stage, a dual-purpose hall and church, was dedicated in October 1956. Canon Dudley Hodges, The Bishop of Lichfield, and F.W. Carder are offered tea by Revd Peter Wylde, the priest in charge.

Holy Trinity, Baswich, 1926 (E. Leigh). The old church was almost entirely rebuilt in 1740. The nave was demolished and rebuilt in red brick, round-headed windows were inserted into the chancel and the top of the medieval tower was rebuilt.

Holy Trinity interior, Baswich, 1966 (M. Peters). Most of the interior fittings seen here date from 1740. Much of the chancel was occupied by two magnificent family pews. On the south side, this pew or gallery for the Chetwyns of Brocton was raised on stout pillars and reached by the staircase beyond the pillars. The family sat all round their gallery and even had their own fireplace. On the north side was a similar gallery for the Levetts of Milford Hall. Recently other changes have been made.

St Thomas', Walton-on-the-Hill, 1928
(G. Pierce). In the nineteenth century Walton-on-the-Hill was an outlying part of the parish of Baswich and a long way from the parish church. St Thomas' was built as a chapel of ease. In 1845, two years after its opening, the spire was destroyed by lightning and replaced by this wooden spire covered in lead.

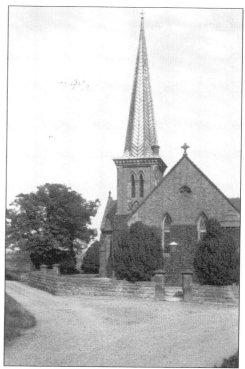

St Thomas' interior, Walton-on-the-Hill, 1926 (E. Leigh). The memorial on the left commemorates Lieutenant R.B. Levett of Milford Hall, who was killed in action in 1917, aged nineteen. The lectern, in the form of an angel, was given in memory of his grandmother. The church with its suspended oil lamps and candles in wall brackets was always dark. In 1930, when electricity was installed, much of the wall decoration seen on this postcard, published by Radford Bank post office, was removed.

All Saints, Sandon, 1995. The interior of Sandon church makes an immediate impression with its seventeenth-century bleached oak pews, carved chancel screen and gallery, and other seventeenth-century furnishings and tombs. The gallery is the family pew of the Harrowby family from Sandon Hall. The large monument in the chancel is dedicated to Samson Erdeswick, the antiquarian, who filled the windows with heraldic glass and painted family trees on the north wall.

St Chad's, Seighford, 1920 (W.H Smith & Son). The tower of the church collapsed around 1610 and was rebuilt in brick, as were the walls damaged when it fell. The rest of the church is unspoilt medieval work with a Norman arcade and chancel arch seen above. The pulpit and altar rails date from the seventeenth century. The stained glass window in the centre of this postcard is in memory of Colonel Frederick Eld of Seighford Hall, and the church is full of memorials to the Elds and other families.

The Church Army van, 1928 (A. Guy). This van was used for missions to parishes in the diocese of Lichfield. It is seen here outside Christ Church vicarage during a visit to Stafford in May 1928. Father Shawcross, vicar of Christ Church, is on the far right. The two female missioners are Sister Birch and Sister Pates.

Zion Chapel, 1966 (M. Peters). In 1811 the Congregationalists in Stafford built a new chapel in Martin Street. The new building cost over £1,000 and was far too large. Bankruptcy was only avoided because of a loan from Thomas Birch of Armitage. Later, attendances increased and Zion Chapel was given a new façade (see p. 70). In 1965 the chapel was sold to Staffordshire County Council and a new one built in Eastgate Street. This is the interior during demolition.

Thomas Russell, 1853. Thomas Russell was born at Middlewich in 1806 and became a travelling Primitive Methodist preacher at an early age. In 1835 he came to live at Lane End in Longton. From there he preached in Stafford where he 'laid a foundation for perpetuity'. He left the area in 1838. Some of his personal possessions are now at Englesea Brook Museum of Primitive Methodism.

Primitive Methodist Chapel, Stafford, 1962 (M. Peters). The congregation started by Thomas Russell met in a room at the north end of Stafford until their first chapel was opened in New Street. In 1849 it was replaced by this larger chapel on Snow Hill, at the southern end of Gaol Road. The chapel closed in 1958 and was being used as a warehouse when this photograph was taken. It was demolished in 1968.

Interior of Primitive Methodist Chapel, Snow Hill, Stafford, 1930. In the 1880s the Revd W. Turner launched an appeal to add rooms for a Sunday school at the back of the chapel and to refurbish the interior. The chapel was completely redecorated, given a new floor and seating, and the furnishings re-varnished. It was said to have changed from a dull place to being 'convenient, attractive and cheerful'. Each pew had a small card, just visible in this picture, bearing the name of the family that sat there.

The Jubilee Chapel, Gnosall, 1929. The Primitive Methodists built this chapel in 1901. It replaced an earlier chapel on the other side of the road, which was converted into a private school, before being pulled down and a modern house built on the site. The car is parked outside Jessop's drug store which was 'licensed to sell patent medicines, methylated spirits and tobacco'.

The Wesleyan Chapel, Stafford, 1954. The Wesleyan Methodists built a plain brick chapel on this site in Mount Street in 1811. By the 1860s the roof had developed serious defects and in 1863 this more imposing chapel was opened on the same site. A house for the minister was built next to it. The chapel remained in use until compulsorily acquired and demolished for the redevelopment of St John's Market in the 1980s. Only the tower remains today.

The Presbyterian Meeting House, Stafford, 1945 (P. Rogers). The town's first Presbyterian meeting house was built in Sarah Salte's garden in Balk Passage, off Chell Road, in 1674. The building was altered several times and in 1901 a tower was added and the meeting house extended over what had been a graveyard. This view, taken from the top of the gasometer in Chell Road, shows the rear of the meeting house with Mount Street in the background.

The second Baptist church, Water Street, Stafford, 1945 (M. Peters). In 1857 a group with Baptist views withdrew from the Congregational church and met in the Lyceum Theatre. Their first chapel in Water Street was rebuilt using white brick in 1864. This second chapel was replaced by the present chapel on The Green in 1896. By the 1940s the old chapel in Water Street was being used as a grain store with a hoist built onto the front. It was demolished in 1970.

St Patrick's Roman Catholic church, Stafford, 1953. A mass centre to serve the northern suburbs of Stafford was opened at St Patrick's School in 1884 and the first church in St Patrick's Street in 1895. In 1921 Father Kelly acquired a site for a new church and school in Sandon Road. The school opened in 1930 and a hall attached to it was used as a church until the present church was opened in 1953. This photograph shows the church nearing completion.

The Procession of Our Lady, 1923 (A. Guy). In May 1923 Father Kelly organized a Catholic procession through Stafford in honour of the Blessed Virgin Mary. The procession included school children, priests from nearby parishes and members of the congregations of St Patrick's and St Austin's churches, as well as the Children of Mary, seen here in their blue cloaks with white veils, carrying a statue of Our Lady on their shoulders. The procession started from St Patrick's Street and made its way to St Austin's church.

Interior of St Austin's, Stafford, 1912 (Marshall, Keene & Co.). The third Roman Catholic church on this site in Wolverhampton Road was built in 1862. The interior was largely refurbished at the end of the nineteenth century and this picture shows the church as it was soon afterwards. The altar and reredos date from 1884 and statues of John Fisher and Thomas More, presented by Francis Whitgreave of Burton Manor, stand each side of the altar. The oak pulpit was presented in memory of Canon Acton, the priest at St Austin's.

St Paul's School, Stafford, 1910. These pupils, posed outside their school, are around eleven years old. Stiff Eton collars and high-buttoned jackets are worn by most of the boys but the girls are wearing pinafores, dresses and even an early gymslip. Every pupil made an effort to appear smartly turned out as having his or her photograph taken was a special occasion.

Tenterbanks Infant School, Stafford, 1922. The wall calendar suggests that it is May and the teacher has brightened her classroom by sticking colourful cut-out flowers to the dark tiles at the back of the classroom. Round the walls are rhymes: 'Rain Rain, go away'; 'She has eight little fingers'; 'Ladybird, ladybird'; 'Hickory, dickory, dock'; and 'Little Bo-Peep'. The children have a variety of simple craftwork on their desks.

St Lawrence's School, Gnosall, late 1920s. Mid-nineteenth-century schools had a single schoolroom where the head teacher supervised the whole school while pupil teachers taught groups under his supervision. When the idea of a teacher having his or her own classroom spread in the late nineteenth century, glazed folding partitions, like this one at the old St Lawrence's School were a practical way of adapting buildings while retaining the large rooms for some purposes.

Violin lesson at Corporation Street School, Stafford, 1950s. Before the Second World War, the Staffordshire Education Committee was proud that not a single piano in schools had been bought with ratepayers' money. After the war this changed. In 1947 Maude Smith was appointed as the county's first music organizer and slowly schools became more musically active. In 1949 a peripatetic teacher was appointed to introduce violin playing into Stafford schools. This class of beginners was one of the results.

The Great Hall, King Edward VI Grammar School, 1930 (Marshall, Keene & Co.). The new wing of the school, opened by Lord Harrowby in December 1928, faced Friars Road and was linked to the older school buildings by the Great Hall which added to the appearance of the school as well as providing a fine setting for school assemblies. However, it had poor acoustics and failed to provide adequately for a thriving drama tradition. The hall is seen here being used for the annual School Certificate Examination.

Queen Victoria's Diamond Jubilee school celebration, 1897 (D. Bordley). In the afternoon of Jubilee Day over 5,000 children assembled in Market Square in Sunday school groups. After the firebell on the Guild Hall had rung for silence, the children sang the first verse of the National Anthem and gave three cheers for the Queen, the Mayor and the local MP, who had paid for their tea. Everyone then marched off to Stafford Common for tea and to be entertained by Punch and Judy shows, marionettes, air balloons and daylight fireworks.

# *Four*

# Industry

Mason & Marson, clicking department, 1906. Fred Cull of the Australian shoe manufacturers George Cull & Son spent some months working at the Sandon Road factory of Mason & Marson, the English agents for his father's company. This photographic postcard was sent to his wife in November 1906, after they had returned to Sydney. It shows the clicking department where the various parts of the shoe were cut out ready to be made up. The message on the back reads, 'On the rail in front you will notice some of our "Reliable" infant shoes'.

Mason & Marson, closing department, 1906. This picture and the next three are taken from postcards sent to Mrs Cull from Mason & Marson. This is the closing department where the uppers of boots and shoes were sewn together.

Mason & Marson, lasting department, 1906. In this department the uppers were stretched over lasts before the sole and heel were added. On the left, some ladies shoes can be seen on lasts. Spare lasts are hung from the ceiling. Other workers have crowded into the back of the room and posed for this photograph.

Mason & Marson, finishing department, 1906. After leaving the lasting department, the edges of the soles were trimmed, and the heels and soles burnished. In 1906 this was all done by hand.

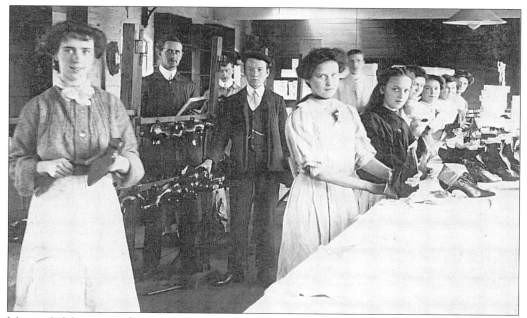

Mason & Marson, packing department, 1906. The shoes were given a final polish, wrapped in tissue paper and boxed before being sent to the stockroom. This was the last postcard in the series sent to Mrs Cull. Each year her husband sent £250 to Mr Marson to spend on a Christmas treat for old people in Stafford. He also promoted Stafford in various ways in Australia. In the 1920s Cull Avenue, Stafford, was named in his honour.

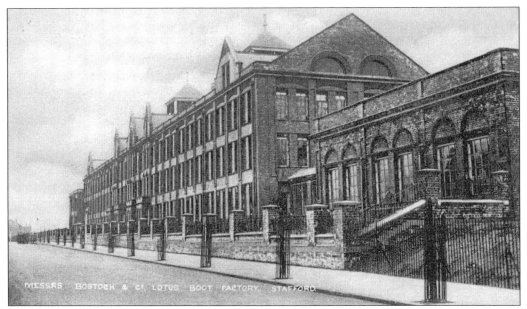

Bostock's factory, 1910 (R. Dawson). Bostock's original shoe factory was in Foregate Street. When it burnt down in 1901 this new factory was built in Sandon Road. J.J. Hays, a local man who had emigrated to America, was brought in to introduce the latest American ideas in production and technology. In the new factory the making of shoes was divided into more processes, each carried out by specialist machinery, and the scale of production was much increased. Bostock's became Lotus in 1919 and closed in 1999, when this factory was demolished.

Lotus' leather warehouse, 1920s. This, and the following four pictures, are part of a series showing the Lotus factory in the 1920s. Here, the different types of leather used in the factory are being inspected and sorted.

Lotus' closing room, 1920s. Compare this picture with that of sewing shoe uppers at Mason & Marson twenty years earlier (p. 102). The difference in the scale of manufacture is obvious. Note the new fashion for short hair which has been adopted by most of the women.

Lotus' lasting department, 1920s. This stage of manufacture has been divided into a number of processes, each carried out by specialist machinery. Shoes are stacked on trolleys and wheeled from one machine to the next by young boys.

Lotus' packing department, 1920s. Each trolley was loaded with one style and size of shoe. These were wrapped in pairs and put into boxes which were properly labelled. Note that in all these pictures foremen and forewomen are distinguished from other workers by their dress. In this picture the foreman is the only one wearing a collar and tie.

Lotus' office, 1920s. In the nineteenth century this would have been a room full of male clerks. The invention of what Remington advertised as 'the machine to supersede the pen' provided a whole new range of job opportunities for women and by the 1920s many offices had an all-female staff. Note the old-fashioned two-piece telephone between the second and third clerks on the left.

Dutch dancing at Lotus, 1920s. After the First World War Lotus appointed Miss Thompson as its first welfare superintendent to develop the social side of its factory. The company laid out playing fields, held an annual sports day, began a bowling club and ran a dramatic society. They also encouraged employees to take part in a number of gymnastic activities, including what the anonymous photographer called 'Dutch dancing'.

Lotus' closing room, 1937. The girls in the factory had always been encouraged to decorate floats and individual entries, such as bicycles, for the Stafford Infirmary pageant. In 1937 they used their expertise to decorate the closing room for the Coronation of King George VI.

Glacia Salt Works, 1970. Brine deposits were discovered accidentally beneath Stafford Common in 1877 during the search for a water supply for the town. The discovery was not exploited until 1893 when local businessmen formed The Stafford Salt & Alkali Co. and began producing salt near Stafford Common station. Other works followed. In the 1960s pumping brine caused subsidence at the north end of the town and further pumping was banned in 1970. This is The British Soda Company's Glacia Salt Works in Common Road.

Stoking salt furnaces, Chance & Hunt, 1914. Brine was pumped into large shallow pans and the water evaporated by furnaces beneath them. These are the furnaces below the pans. Chance & Hunt were a Wednesbury company who took over Winston Bros' saltworks on Stafford Common in 1907. The old Stafford Fever Hospital became their manager's house.

Filling salt tubs, 1914. Damp salt was shovelled from the open pans into these elm tubs, which were allowed to stand until any surplus water had drained through slots in the bottom. The tubs were then turned upside down and carefully removed to leave blocks of salt. These were wheeled into the hothouse to dry.

Packing salt, 1914. The lumps of salt were taken from the hothouse and cut into blocks with a circular saw, before being packed for sale. Until 1914 most salt for use in the home was sold in blocks. It was only later that free running salt in packets was produced in Stafford.

W.G. Bagnall Ltd, 1927. W.G. Bagnall built his first locomotive in 1876 at his Castle Street works alongside the main railway line. In its early years the company built many small locomotives and waggons for quarries and light services abroad. Around 1914 the works were extended to enable larger locomotives to be built. These pictures show part of the machine shop (above) and the wheel bay (below).

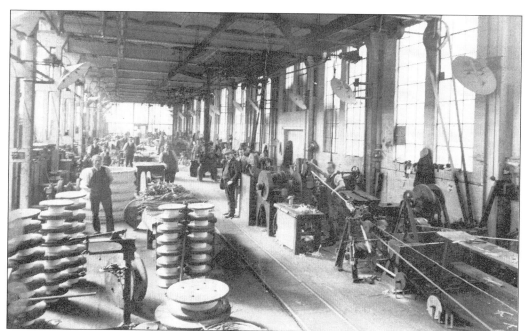

The English Electric Co., c. 1925. Siemens' Dynamo Works was opened in 1903 after the company relocated from Woolwich. As well as building generators and electric motors, the factory also built a wide variety of other electrical appliances. The Siemens brothers were German and because of this the factory was taken over by the Government in 1914. After the war it became part of The English Electric Company, a merger of several companies. These 1920s photographs show coil winding (above) and non-ferrous casting by the green sand process (below).

Making tanks, English Electric Co., 1944. On the outbreak of war in 1939, the English Electric Co. changed to war work. Part of the factory began to make tanks for the Army. In 1944 they had an order for 300 heavy cruiser Comet tanks. These weighed 32 tons, had a crew of 5, and were armed with a 17lb 97mm gun. This tank is almost complete and is being fitted with 18in wide tracks.

Testing a Comet tank, 1944. The Comet was an all-welded tank and, when completed, had to be tested in this water dip excavated at the English Electric factory to be sure it was watertight. The tank would then be given its final tests on Cannock Chase before going into service.

HM Submarine *Visigoth*, 1944. The English Electric Co. adopted this submarine during the war. Books, games, parcels and letters were sent regularly by the company and its employees. In February 1944 the captain and a number of his crew were invited to spend a weekend staying with employees in Stafford. The programme for the visit included a tour of the factory, a dance, the presentation of an inscribed Bible and having this photograph taken of the captain and crew with members of the organizing committee.

Spic & Span Shoe Polishes Ltd, 1932. The company was established in 1932 to make floor and shoe polishes in this factory in Glover Street. In 1938 Dr H. Simon joined the company, which then diversified into chemical waterproofing products, adhesives and sealants. In 1940 the company was renamed Evode Chemical Works Ltd and in 1954 moved to a new factory in Common Road.

The gasworks, Chell Road, 1953 (P. Rogers). The town's first gasworks were built here in 1829. The company was bought by the Borough Council in 1878 and the plant taken over by the West Midland Gas Board in 1949. By that time none of the original works remained. This was the view from the top of No. 5 gas holder with Broadeye Mill on the far right. The area was cleared in the late 1960s and is now the site of Wilkinson's and car parks.

# *Five*
# Some Special Occasions

Queen Victoria's Diamond Jubilee, Stafford, 1897 (D. Bordley). The centre piece of the second day of celebrations was the roasting of two oxen, given by Mr Meakin of Cresswell Hall, in Market Square. The fire was lit at 10.00 p.m. on Tuesday and the carcasses turned slowly and basted regularly all night. The first slices were cut at 9.00 a.m. on Wednesday and given out with bread. By noon all the oxen was gone and four sheep were roasted on the spits. Beer donated by local brewers was also available by ticket.

Queen Victoria's Diamond Jubilee celebrations, first day, 1897 (D. Bordley). The Borough Council provided no street decorations for the Jubilee but the Guild Hall and its windows were outlined with coloured lights. Jubilee Day, a Tuesday, was a public bank holiday and the celebrations in Stafford got off to a poor start when it was discovered that the Mayor's mace was in a bank vault and the bank closed for the day. However, the Volunteers and their band led a parade round the town and then formed up below the Guild Hall to fire three blank cartridges in a *feu de joie*. The Jubilee was the first occasion in the town to be officially photographed. David Bordley took this photograph on Tuesday morning, pictures of the children's celebration on Tuesday afternoon (see p. 100) and pictures of the ox-roast early Wednesday morning (see p. 115). Notice the fire bell on the Guild Hall roof. During the second Burmese War in 1852, the Staffordshire Volunteers captured the Green Dragon Pagoda in Rangoon and some of them decided to loot one of its bells. The 200lb trophy was smuggled home and later presented to the borough.

Visit by Edward VII, 1907. In 1907 Edward VII, at the end of a visit to Lord Shrewsbury at Ingestre, drove through Stafford and agreed to stop briefly in Market Square. The town was profusely decorated. In Market Square the Volunteers' Band played while the Mayor and councillors waited on the Shire Hall steps. The King's car, with a pilot car in front, drew up and he was briefly welcomed by the Mayor before being driven off.

Old people's breakfast, 1911. In Stafford George V's Coronation Day began with a breakfast for 780 people over 60 years of age in the Market Hall. During the meal the Borough Military Band played and afterwards the guests were entertained by Stafford Glee Club. Those present received either an ounce of tobacco or 1 lb of tea with a portrait of the King and Queen, as a gift from the MP for the borough.

Gnosall Wakes Week, 1906 (Midland Photo Co.). Wakes Week with its parade of Foresters, club feasts and pony riding at The Oak was always in mid-August. In 1906 a committee was formed to add a sports day to the attractions. The sports meeting was held in a field next to the railway station. The first event was a 'go-as-you-please' walking race, starting on the road by the station and going three times round Gnosall and Gnosall Heath. This was followed by a variety of races and jumps, and a tug-of-war.

Fancy Dress Competition, 1906 (H. Osbourne). Sports day at Gnosall ended with an event called 'goose-jingling' and competitions for the best ladies' fancy costume, which Mrs A. Webb won as Britannia, and the most comical gentlemen's outfit, which Mr F. Mears won as The Belle of Gnosall.

Gnosall Sports Day, 1906 (F. Mears). Hot weather made for thirsty competitors and watchers. A local publican placed his barrels in a shady spot next to the sports field and did a thriving trade. The photographer was later the winner of the most comical gentlemen's outfit competition.

Gnosall Sports Day, 1909 (H. Osbourne). In 1909 a sheep given by Mr D. Hall of London was roasted and cut up while the races took place. Later, eighteen poor widows and parishioners lined up behind the table with their baskets before the meat was distributed.

Gustav Hamel at Stafford, 1912 (A. Guy). This 'Grand Flying Exhibition at Lammascote by the World's Greatest Flyer, Mr Gustav Hamel,' was arranged by Martin Mitchell (see p. 22). The 50hp Bleriot monoplane arrived at Stafford by rail. On the day of the display 3,500 people paid a shilling to watch Hamel 'rival the aerial revels of the mythical witch on a broomstick'. Before the first of several flights, Hamel and Martin Mitchell (standing with one hand on the monoplane) posed for this picture.

Funeral procession at Stafford, 1908 (J. Vandyke). This untitled picture is almost certainly the funeral of Major J.E. Knight, son of Dr Edward Knight who was a physician at the Staffordshire General Infirmary. He joined the Yeomanry in 1848 and spent his whole life with the army, becoming second-in-command and musketry instructor of the Staffordshire Militia before he retired to live at Camden Place on Wolverhampton Road. His military-style funeral is led by the band of the militia with muffled drums.

Farewell to New Zealand troops, 1919 (C. Fowke). Before the troops left their camp on Cannock Chase at the end of the First World War, an official farewell was planned. A silk Union Jack and New Zealand Ensign were presented to them in Market Square. The troops then marched to Siemens' sports field. On the way the Mayor, J. Rushton, took the salute on a dais erected outside the public library. In this picture the dais is half hidden by a New Zealand Ensign.

New Zealand troops' sports meeting, 1919 (C. Fowke). After the ceremony in Market Square and the march past, the troops held their brigade sports on Siemens' sports ground, watched by a large number of the public. This is the final of the tug-of-war in which Wellington beat an Otago team.

Peace Day, Stafford, 1919 (C. Fowke). The peace treaty to end the First World War was signed in June 1919 and 19 July was set aside as Peace Day 'to celebrate victory and commemorate those who had overthrown the menace of a great enemy'. The Borough Military Band gave an afternoon concert for the crowds who came to Victoria Park.

Peace Day, Stafford, 1919 (C. Fowke). The Duds Concert Party, seen here on the right in pierrot costume, also entertained the crowds in Victoria Park. In the evening the Borough Council had arranged a water carnival on the Sow and, in the park, dancing to the Borough Military Band and a firework display. Unfortunately, heavy rain in the early evening caused all these to be postponed.

Children celebrate peace, Stafford, 1919 (C. Fowke). On the day before Peace Day, all the school children in Stafford were given a tea in their own school and then taken to Stafford Common for a fête. Various attractions had been arranged including Punch and Judy in a striped kiosk on the left. In the evening, adults joined their children for dancing and the event ended with 'fire-balloons and rockets'.

Opening of David Hollin Nurses' Home, 1927 (C. Fowke). David Hollin, a shoe manufacturer, left a large sum in his will to build a home for twenty-eight nurses in Foregate Street, next to the infirmary. The Nurses' Home was officially opened by Prince Henry, later Duke of Gloucester, who arrived by car from Sandon Hall. He is seen here outside the new Nurses' Home with Lord Stafford, Mayor W.T. Richardson and the Town Clerk, waiting for the official photographer.

Prince of Wales at Stafford, 1924 (C. Fowke). In June 1924 the Prince of Wales, later Edward VIII, made a brief stop at Stafford on his return journey from north Staffordshire by train. A temporary platform decorated in red, white and blue was erected outside the station and fifty ex-servicemen formed up in front of it. The Prince was presented with a pink carnation buttonhole by Mrs Wheeldon, the Mayor's wife, before his official welcome and an inspection of the ex-servicemen.

The Stafford pageant, 1909. The Trades and Friendly Societies' Pageant, with its parade of decorated vehicles and pedestrians, took place in Stafford every summer. Prizes were awarded for the best decorated entries in a variety of categories. Along the route collections were made for the Staffordshire General Infirmary. In 1909 the winning trade tableau was 'Old Style Shoemaking', entered by the employees of R. Podmore, and seen here passing The Royal Brine Baths.

Stafford Infirmary Pageant, 1919 (T. Hipwell). Every year the employees of the Lotus factory provided many entries in the infirmary pageant. Departments in the factory vied with each other to produce the most striking display. Above is 'Rose Queen' entered in the name of P. Clewes and F. Bailey in 1919 and winner of a second prize.

Baby Day, 1927. After the First World War, the Maternity and Child Welfare Committee of the council organized an annual Baby Day with prizes for decorated prams. Entrants paraded their prams along the main street and finished in Victoria Park, where judging took place. In 1927 Baby Day had to be held in the Market Hall due to bad weather. The prizewinners were Mrs Rees of Cross Street and Mrs Lees of Oxford Gardens who won the prams decorated with artificial flowers category; Mrs Denning of Railway Terrace who won the prams decorated with real flowers category; and Mrs Banner of Fairway who won the mail cart category.

The Great Balloon Race, 1930s (A. Guy). The race was held to raise money for the infirmary. Each balloon had a label and the finder was asked to return it with a note of where the balloon had been found. Cash prizes of up to £1 were donated by the Mayor and the council. Weekly lists of long distance returns were printed in the local press. The race formally opened when the Mayor signalled to the Mayoress and other ladies to release the first five balloons in Market Square.

VE Day party, 1945. The end of the war in Europe was celebrated by children's street parties in many parts of Stafford. This one was in North Castle Street. Before everyone sat down to a tea party in Bagnall's canteen, the Mayor and Mayoress, Mr and Mrs Wallace Copeland, judged the fancy dress competition. First prize went to Carol Woollams (left) as The Angel of Peace. Others in the front row are Trevor and Marlene Cook, Jean Follows and Armand Chatfield.

General de Gaulle at Stafford, 1941. In October 1941 General de Gaulle, leader of the Free French Forces and a tank expert, visited the English Electric factory to see tanks being made. At the factory, a guard of honour was drawn from the works' Home Guard Company. The General is shown shaking hands with Joseph Sabin. He noticed one of the Home Guard, Reg Lloyd, was wearing the ribbon of the French Croix-de-Guerre from the First World War.

Queen Mother at Lotus, 1953. The Queen Mother officially opened the Blithfield Reservoir in October 1953 and then, after lunch at Blithfield Hall, drove to the Lotus factory in Stafford. She was received at the Freeman Street entrance by James Bostock the managing director. After starting up a new closing room conveyor, she toured the factory. Here, she is talking to Alice Hodson, forewoman of the bow section. James Bostock is half hidden behind her and the Lord Lieutenant of the County is on the right.